Independent Wealth:
How to Start an Online Business in 5 Steps

Turn your passion into passive income

Front Matter

Copyright and Disclosures

Copyright © 2020 Get Up Stand Up Enterprises, Ltd.

Independent Wealth: Start an Online Business in 5 Steps. Turn Your Passion into Passive Income, Joe France

Book One of "The Independent You Series."

www.theindependentyou.com

ISBN: 9798686962460

All rights reserved. No part of this publication may be reproduced, stored in a retrieval system, or transmitted, in any form or by any means, electronic, mechanical, photocopying, recording or otherwise without prior written permission from the publisher. The author and publisher of the book do not make any claim or guarantee for any physical, mental, emotional, spiritual, or financial result. All products, services, and information provided by the author are for general education and entertainment purposes only. The information provided herein is in no way a substitute for professional advice. In the event you use any of the information contained in this book for yourself, the author and publisher will have no liability.

Acknowledgments

For my family – who let me do me

To Steve and Julie – my editorial team

And to my parents – my most generous supporters

Foreword

I'm guessing if you have picked this book up, you're probably trying to find out how to start an online business. Some time ago, I looked for the same information, and it wasn't easy to find; and I already had a lengthy background in online technology. After a great deal of searching and trial and error, I pieced things together and found a way that worked. I didn't have to raise any money; I leveraged my time to cover my costs and fund my ideas. And I built an independent online business that generates passive income, the foundation for independent wealth.

In this book, I will show you:

- How to start your own business step by step
- The keys to making money from popular activities:
    - Podcasting
    - Stock footage
    - Online courses
    - Blogging
    - E-commerce
- How to start a home business in 2020

- What the best online entrepreneur courses are
- How to generate passive income doing what you love

When I was very young, I loved to read. I had read all the books in my parents' library by the age of 14, and I dreamed of becoming a writer. But, as often happens to young people, I was influenced by naysayers, who told me I wouldn't make money being a writer. I didn't come from a wealthy family, so I took their words to heart. I decided not to become a writer until I made money first. I suppressed that part of me and set about trying to make money as quickly as I could. I chose online technology because that seemed like an excellent way to do that. After 20 years, I had experienced many highs and lows, but I still hadn't become a writer.

This book is about the process I used to turn my dream to become a writer into an online business that generates passive income and independent wealth. I made mistakes along the way, so I want to share what worked and what didn't, to save time and make the process easier for others. I hope it will help you to become independent doing what you love, too.

Table of Contents

Front Matter ii

Acknowledgments iii

Foreword... iv

Introduction: All that glitters is not gold viii

Chapter One: Dawn of the Web and the Online Entrepreneur 1

Chapter Two: The Penny Begins to Drop 6

Chapter Three: How to Start an Online Business in Five Steps 11

    Step One: First, Choose Your Passion 11

    Step Two: Freelance Your Passion 15

    Step Three: Choose Your Enterprise 22

    Step Four: Know Your Own Story 40

    Step Five: Find Your Online Tribe 43

Chapter Four: Beyond the Side Hustle 50

Conclusion: If You Can Imagine It, You Can Do It 53

References 55

About the Author 59

Introduction: All that glitters is not gold

In 2019, after more than two decades of working in the online tech industry, I decided to start my own online business. I had some ideas about what I did and didn't want to do. I wanted to be independent; I didn't want to work for someone else's company anymore. I didn't want to hire staff because I know what a big responsibility it is to employ people. That meant a business I could do by myself, not a tech company like those I had worked in before. I had a young family, so I did need to make money, at least enough to replace the senior salaries I had earned previously. I didn't have a lot of money to invest, though, so I could only start something that wouldn't require much capital. I wanted to love whatever I did because I knew I would be spending a significant amount of time on it.

I gave myself this challenge at the beginning, and this book is the result.

"Water, water, everywhere, nor any drop to drink."[i]

One thing you will find at the start is there is so much information out there, but no blueprint for how to create a profitable company. It was tough to work everything out, even for someone with experience in online technology.

On YouTube, there are millions of hours of videos on almost every aspect of online business, all free. They only feature specific business models, though, like podcasting or e-commerce, and the information is all in bits and pieces. YouTube is just one channel; there's also Google search results page, blogs by the thousands, podcasts, and forum chats. And, of course, Facebook.

I was bombarded by advertisements promoting "secret" solutions, inviting me to buy an online course or e-book. They use a technique called "click funnels." When someone enters an email address, they receive offers for e-books, courses, and products. They appear persistently in their email inbox and across social media.

How could anyone verify what is true? Or know what is right for them? Create a business plan? Even if you could connect the information from all the different sources, you have no idea how long it might take to generate an income—if at all.

No wonder so many people choose to keep their day job.

If at first you don't succeed, try, try again

While working at agile tech companies, I learned that sometimes testing is the best way to discover. Without more information to go on, I decided to try some of the models myself, starting with "drop-shipping."

This kind of online store looks like any other, but the products it sells are held by a third party, which sends a purchased product to the customer. It is simplified e-commerce without the headaches of managing inventory and shipping. The idea sounded good, and there were many positive stories about how much money you can earn. I set up a WordPress website with a connection to Alibaba: a marketplace for millions of goods made in China. I designed a niche shop, with products for shaving and men's grooming. I even started to work on the store's branding.

At this point, though, I discovered how much money you need to spend on Facebook advertising, and not just at the start. Anybody can buy the products directly from Alibaba, so there is no competitive advantage. To make a drop-shipping store successful, you need to spend time and money on paid advertising to bring in customers. I calculated that if my sales revenue were double my ad spend, I would still have to pay $50,000 for every $100,000 in revenue. Then subtract other costs before earning "income." And I knew from experience how hard it is to generate a 2x return on advertising spend.

I learned that the people who are successful at drop-shipping open multiple stores and try hundreds of different products. There are many moving parts that I didn't think through at the start, such as the payment process, returns policy, and terms and conditions, to mention a few. I quickly realized that running and managing an online store wasn't what I wanted to do, even if it could make money. And certainly not if I had to invest thousands (or hundreds of thousands) in advertising to do it.

Back to the drawing board…

I spent some time investigating Google Maps, which I knew was being used more and more as a search engine, especially to find local businesses. Advertising is still at an early stage in Maps compared to Google's main search page. I planned to create a service to help local companies appear in searches and acquire new customers. I found a company that sells a platform to manage this advertising, but it was $5,000 to sign up. I moved on quickly.

Then I tried creating a course for people on how to start an online business. I saw so many advertisements for courses on "how to build online courses," but as I went further into it, I saw that you need to pay for advertising, too. And depending on the price you charge for the course, you might need to do a lot of selling. I didn't want to get back into sales again.

I tested and researched for several months, and I noticed a pattern amongst all the noise. There seemed to be two different approaches to making money online: the "side hustle" and the "passion" approaches is how I started to think of them. In a side hustle, people start and change activity quickly if they don't make money. The people who build a business around their passion are fewer in number but more interesting for me. I knew from experience that doing something you love makes you more successful.

Chapter One: Dawn of the Web and the Online Entrepreneur

I calculated once that if I have worked on average 50 hours a week, with two to three weeks holiday a year, for more than 20 years, then I have logged 50,000 hours at the online technology coal face. Maybe I took a few more holidays, but on the other hand, I probably worked more than 50 hours a week. You get my point, anyway.

When I look back, it was an incredible ride from the early embryonic days of the worldwide web to the Internet of Things today. The blueprint for starting an online business that I discovered (and am sharing with you in this book) has been shaped by truly authentic experiences—the good, the bad, and the occasionally ugly!

Learning the online tech ropes in Asia

I joined my first startup in Tokyo in 1999. I loved the fast pace and decided that startups were my thing. I hadn't worked for a big company before and knew now that I never would. When I joined, the company was just five people. The basic service we provided was connecting office networks for foreign companies in Tokyo. We helped Virgin Cinemas,

Goldman Sachs, and many other foreign companies open their offices in Tokyo.

A few years later, I moved to Bangkok, Thailand, and joined another very early stage online tech startup. There were only seven or eight people in the beginning, but we grew to 260 in just a couple of years. We opened more than a dozen different companies, which was enough to make your head spin. One business ran the local MSN portal and sold advertising into Hotmail and Messenger when they were still popular. Another company sold Google Search. Then Facebook suddenly became popular in Bangkok; it had the highest percentage of Facebook users of any city in the world at one point.

My primary project was to build an online ad network, which is where I first got to see how audiences work online. In the early 2000s, advertisers and their agencies were still phoning websites to book banner placements, paying on a weekly or monthly basis. We worked out a plan to link hundreds of Southeast Asian websites in a platform for automated advertising. We named it Admax, which we thought was pretty cool at the time. We borrowed heavily from the ideas of Silicon Valley, especially startups with even cooler names, like The Rubicon Project and Tribal Fusion.

In 2005 I flew with a co-founder to San Francisco to meet Tribal Fusion's founder, Dilip DaSilva, to ask if we could partner with him in Asia. He laughed and said that he planned to do it by himself. Admax did win that battle in Southeast Asia, but Dilip's network was much more successful than ours in the end.

Despite some early wins, our technology wasn't as advanced as online ad networks in the US; it didn't track everything they could. Machine learning was already developing, and we were a long way from having anything like that. But we had hundreds of websites onboard, and they appreciated the revenue we sent them. Admax was later sold for a bit over $20 million.

The highs and lows of an entrepreneurial life

In 2009, I was offered the chance to sell my shares and jumped at it. I had achieved a personal milestone and felt that I had finally "made it." Then I was convinced by another entrepreneur to take my earnings and invest them in his technology startup. This time it was golf technology. As you can see, I have never been scared to try things.

I thought I was going into a "lifestyle business," where I would get to play golf every day, but I had jumped out of the frying pan and into the fire. Overexcited by some early success, we grew the company too quickly. I was soon working harder than ever, building indoor golf centers, selling memberships, and trying to create a golf coaching app. Our revenue never caught up with our costs, and we struggled to break even. After four years of trying, we admitted defeat and started the painful process of winding down the company, selling off the assets, and laying off staff.

It was a hard lesson to learn. In what seemed like just a few steps, I managed to lose everything I had earned in the last ten years. I was devastated and exhausted but couldn't afford to take the time to process it. My wife and I had recently welcomed our third child, and our costs were trending upward significantly, especially since schools in Bangkok are crazy expensive.

Learning all about machine learning

Not long after that, I met a person who said he had opened up a company called "Taboola" in the Asia Pacific. I had already seen their logo on many websites and spent hours clicking on "Content You May Like." I knew something was going on with the technology, so in 2014, I joined yet another startup.

At that stage, Taboola had 150 people worldwide, but there were just six of us for all of Asia. My job was to ask websites to connect to the Taboola platform and find advertisers to spend money on the network. I got to see machine learning first-hand, something that is changing the way the web works now.

It felt like I spent most of the next four years on a plane, as I opened up offices in new countries like Japan, Singapore, and Australia. I still loved the vibe of a technology startup, but it was a tiring lifestyle, especially with young kids at home. So, at the end of 2018, I decided to finally take a break and go back to my native New Zealand with my family.

That is where I found myself in 2019, trying to work out how to build an online business without much startup capital.

Chapter Two: The Penny Begins to Drop

To see how the web has changed, check your credit card statement

As I tried out different models, I noticed one thing that stood out over all the technology advances. Internet users in 2019 were paying for things online. Not just gaming, music, or online shopping. People were now paying for content on podcasts and YouTube channels. They were paying for courses, and they were signing up for all kinds of different memberships. That simply wasn't the case in the 2000s, and not even in the first half of the 2010s.

Back then, advertising was the top way to monetize the web. I knew from the ad network we built that you need an enormous number of page views to make money from advertising. Not just millions of page views — hundreds of millions. Users don't click on advertisements if they can avoid it. It requires repeated advertising impressions for them to click and take action. Until recently, most online business models aimed to generate a massive audience so that advertising could work. Tech entrepreneurs worked on big ideas and grandiose goals. Becoming a "Solopreneur" wasn't very common.

But now, in 2019, I could see individuals earning money from subscriptions, memberships, and course fees. And there were so many platforms where an individual could earn royalties for uploading content. Anyone could make high-quality content, upload it, and get paid. No studio, agent, editor, or any other middleman service required. You could make money now from a smaller audience than when advertising was the primary way to make money online.

What can happen when you do what you love

The other thing I started to become aware of was how many people now were setting up small independent businesses doing something they loved. There were stories about people making radical career changes to follow their passion online and becoming successful.

One example that impressed me was Nagi Maehashi, who lives in Australia. Nagi had been a senior executive in a finance company with a very high income. But her "obsession," as she calls it, was food. Nagi believed she would regret not following her passion. She quit her job and created an online business around food and recipes, starting with a blog called "RecipeTin Eats." She began in 2014, and by 2019, she was making more than $1,000,000 a year from her business[ii].

I knew from my own experience that successful people loved what they were doing. At Taboola, I got to spend time with the founder, Adam Singolda. By 2016, the company was already a "unicorn" —worth more than one billion dollars. Adam had started in 2007, and I was among the hundreds of employees who celebrated its tenth anniversary. I was struck at the time by Adam talking about how much he was looking forward to the next ten years leading the business. At the time, I thought that you better make sure you love what you're doing when you start a business because you might end up spending most of your adult life doing it.

When I looked at my career, I knew I had chosen to work at companies based on how successful that might be and how much I could earn. I thought that was the right way to look at things because I needed to make money first and foremost. I didn't think I could afford just to do what I wanted to do. I don't think I am unusual in this respect. I think society, in general, treats someone who says they are pursuing their passion with suspicion. When we hear that, we naturally assume that person doesn't want to be wealthy. And for a lot of our lives, that was probably true.

Most people haven't caught up yet with the potential to earn money on the web. It offers a myriad of opportunities for people who have a passion but haven't had the chance to pursue it yet. As internet users, we notice small changes every day, but the potential to make money online is still so new. There is very little information about how online business works. The general wisdom is lagging, as it usually does. We intuitively know that more and more people (if not most) in time will earn their primary income online. How to do that isn't common knowledge yet.

As I looked at examples of entrepreneurs starting successful independent small businesses, I could see a chance to change the pattern of my career. Instead of focusing only on money-making potential, I stopped and thought about what I wanted to do. And when I did that, I remembered a decision I had made more than 30 years before.

In high school, I had already developed a passion for writing. I read voraciously, and I loved to write. I could picture the rest of my life as a writer. But it never happened. I was influenced by people who told me that it would be too hard to make money from writing—and there was truth to that. I said to myself that I should get experience and make some money first, and after that, I could devote myself to writing. Then I promptly forgot about making that decision.

I traveled and joined startups, experiencing all of the ups and downs that went with those. I was lucky enough to have a family, which took up a lot of my time and also shaped my priorities. Whenever I thought about writing, I dismissed it. I just assumed I wouldn't be able to make enough money from it. As I looked at the changes in the web, I began to think about what it was I wanted to do with the rest of my life.

Like Nagi Maehashi, when I thought about myself in the future, I knew I would regret not following my writing passion. No amount of money would make up for that. I even started to realize that doing something I didn't love was limiting my capacity to make money anyway. And I could see that the web was offering me a chance to change course. Over the next few months, I worked out a five-step process for setting up an online business that would allow me to write. And a chance to create independent wealth.

Chapter Three: How to Start an Online Business in Five Steps

Step One: First, Choose Your Passion

I knew now that I wanted to start a business where I could write, but I wasn't sure what topic to write about or where to do it. As I researched the ways people can make money online, I learned that some topics are profitable, and some are not. A profitable topic is one where internet users are already paying for products and services. Photography, for example, is an area where people buy lots of related products and take courses. On the other hand, history, something I love to read about, is not a profitable topic because people aren't paying a lot online for related tools, products, or subscriptions.

Here are some examples of profitable topics to make it easier to visualize:

Creative Topics

- Art & Crafts
- Design
- Fashion

- Filmmaking
- Photography

Practical Topics

- Home Renovation & DIY
- Health & Fitness
- Food & Drink
- Parenting

Professional Topics

- Career
- Business
- Leadership
- Marketing
- Finance

This is not an exhaustive list. It's just to give you an idea of the scope. I discovered that choosing to do what you want to do is the first step in building a successful online business. You need to start with something that you just absolutely love to do. Something you are fascinated by and would spend as much time on as you possibly could, regardless of money. If you choose to pursue that and commit to it, there are many ways to make money online from it. The opportunity on the web has reached that point.

As we go through my five-step process, I will share examples of people who are enjoying online business success. At this stage, don't focus on how you will do it or where you can generate money. Starting at those points will lead you in the wrong direction. Even if you are still skeptical, and I understand if you are, just enjoy the exercise of thinking about what you want to do—possibly for the rest of your life!

For some people, this part will be easy. Some of you may have been thinking for a long time now about how you can get to do what you love doing. You might already be skipping to the next part about how to make money from it. For others, you might have an idea, but you're not sure if it is your real passion. The first step, choosing your passion, is easier said than done. Give yourself time to work this out. Don't rush it. I hope you will agree; that it is an excellent problem to have.

How to fund an online startup when you are "capital-light"

When you start your online business, you will quickly discover that there are many things you could spend money on, and the costs add up quickly. Plug-ins for websites, tools for designing, software for managing databases, and email lists are everywhere. It is easy to get carried away and buy things you don't need. And it always takes time for revenue to come in.

As an online tec entrepreneur, I experienced startups where we had no capital, bootstrapping our way as best we could. It was fun for a while, and we certainly worked hard, but it added unusual pressure. We didn't always make the best decisions in those situations. And there were other times where we raised investment, which brought the challenges of investors and shareholding. Somehow when we had money, it didn't always bring out the best in people. For my own independent online business, I wanted to find a better solution.

I chose to limit myself to a startup budget of just $5,000. I only spent on things I needed: I took the computer and phone I already had, bought a cheap monitor, and worked at my kitchen table. I was the only director and shareholder of an online business. But I knew that $5,000 wouldn't last very long. I decided the best way to fund my ideas and cover my living costs in the meantime was to freelance part of my time. As the saying goes, "Time is money."

Step Two: Freelance Your Passion

You might wonder, "why freelance?" when you could keep a day job and start an online business as a "side hustle." Well, the answer is easy. I already knew how hard it was to start writing when I had a day job. To start anything else, for that matter. I have been trying to play the guitar for 35 years now, and I'm still not good at it. I knew that if I was going to make money from writing, I needed to get a lot better at it. And that takes time.

I was impressed by the book *Bounce* by Matthew Syed[iii], which explains the benefits of serious practice. Matthew used table tennis, which was his sport, to show how much time you need to get good at something: 10,000 hours. I don't know if that is the right number or not, but I have always liked it as a starting point. If I could spend 40 hours a week writing, it would take me five years to get to a high level. But if I kept a full-time job, where I knew it would be hard to write for even 15 hours a week, it would take me at least 13 years to get to the same level. Assuming I stuck at it for that long.

I chose freelance work that involved writing over keeping my day job so I could start "clocking my hours." I already had some experience in copywriting and knew I enjoyed it. It is a skill that I knew would help me in the next stage of my business. I focused on technology: a topic I know well and a subject that's hard to make sound simple. I thought the challenge of writing technology copy would be good for me.

Freelancing gave me the independence I wanted, and I got to write a lot. I worked with my clients on their brands and what problems their products were solving, topics in which I am naturally interested. I wrote a lot of copy for emails and websites. I also got into working on social media copy, which was something else I wanted to learn.

Freelancing: the new normal

The opportunities to freelance now are so diverse, and there are so many ways to go about it. In the unusual economy brought about by the coronavirus, working from home has become normal. Many people have lost their jobs and are looking for work. At the same time, many companies are choosing to save costs by getting work done through "virtual" services. This fluid environment is opening up all kinds of opportunities for freelancing work online.

The key is to "freelance your passion." Make sure that the service you offer gives you the chance to practice the thing you love doing for as much of your time as possible. Becoming an Uber driver might let you choose your schedule and earn income, but you won't be honing a craft. Take your passion and use freelancing to build up the 10,000 hours as quickly as you can.

Why You Will Make More Money on a Freelancing Platform

It is easier to freelance today because there are so many online platforms that enable this type of work. LinkedIn, for example, can help you to reach out directly to a network of clients, as I did. I had done this type of business development for a long time so that I could choose easy-going clients. I could agree with them an amount of work that still left me the time I needed to build the other parts of my business.

For some readers, it might not be so easy to reach out directly to clients. Maybe you don't have an existing network that needs the new service you want to offer. This is where the new freelancing platforms are completely changing the game.

The most well-known of these are Fiverr and Upwork, both of which allow freelancers to offer a wide range of services. Dozens of other platforms offer more specialist or niche services. For example, 99 Designs is used for an array of creative services, while Expert 360 specializes in senior-level professional services, like marketing strategy, finance, and consulting.

The big benefit of using freelancing platforms like these is that you can control the amount of work you take on and your schedule. Most of these platforms have a system where prospective clients post a brief, so you can choose what projects to bid for. This way, you can manage the amount of freelancing work you do, leaving yourself ample time to build your business.

The downside of these platforms is that you probably have to accept a lower hourly rate than going client-direct. They are competitive marketplaces. You probably need to match the average hourly rates at least until you get established. The platforms also take a percentage of your income. But they help you get paid by acting as a secure escrow service. They receive the money from the client, often upfront, and hold it for you. Outside these platforms, it can be tough to get paid on time by clients. And sometimes to get paid at all.

Teaching or tutoring is another version of freelancing that works very well for this step in building your online business. One-on-one coaching is an ideal way to learn about the problems and challenges that people face, which will help you in the next stage: developing a passive income. And, of course, there are platforms for teaching and tutoring too. Superprof.com, for example, has 100,000 tutors in the US alone.

If you're not ready to freelance your passion, hit the books!

If you know what your passion is but think you are not good enough yet to charge for it as a freelancer, take a course. Three to six months of the right study will get you to a level where you can set an hourly rate for it. You just need to be good enough to get started; it is okay to get paid to learn things as a freelancer. You sell your time, energy, and attitude, as well as your expertise.

Why some people never choose to freelance over their day job

Choosing to quit a salaried role to take up freelancing is a difficult decision for most people. Often, we think about it as a binary choice: current job, which pays well, versus freelancing, which involves many variables and unknowns. And even though freelancing might mean doing the thing we love, that in itself is often not enough incentive to give up a career. Becoming a freelancer may even seem like a step-down. But what if it was only one step in a much bigger plan? A stepping stone.

By the time I started freelance copywriting, I already knew I wanted to generate passive income by self-publishing books online. But I knew that it would take time, even a year or two, to earn enough money to cover my costs, let alone as much as my previous salaries. So, I saw freelancing as the perfect way to cover my expenses and practice writing at the same time.

Goals: why you should "only" aim to cover your costs

I only aimed to cover my costs at this stage, not replace the income I had earned previously. There was a limit to what I could charge as a new copywriter. If I had used my business strategy experience, I could have made more, but I wouldn't have been writing every day. The main reason, though, for choosing the lower bar of covering my costs, was that I wanted to keep some of my time free to build the other parts of my business. Freelancing was how I would fund my business, but it wasn't the ultimate goal.

I knew a fair bit already about passive income. I knew that earning income from assets like an investment or a rental property are ways wealthy people make money. Some of the tech startups I had helped to build generated passive income from courses and franchises. But it wasn't until I began researching the web in 2019 that I started to see how an individual could generate passive income online. Enough to make a living from, and even to gain financial independence.

Freelance income vs. passive income

Freelancing brings a lot of independence, and I enjoy copywriting. The downside is your income potential is always limited by the amount of time you have. A freelancer can grow their income by increasing hourly rates or charging a fixed fee. Successful freelancers who earn high incomes can outsource work to people and make a profit on that. Ultimately, though, freelancing income is always capped by the number of hours in a day.

I wanted to grow a business that would give me financial independence. It isn't that I want to be rich per se. Instead, I equate financial freedom with having a lot more time to spend on writing. As I developed my blueprint, I saw my goals starting to intersect. Instead of waiting until I had money to write, I could build a company based on writing. And if I could generate passive income, that would lead to independent wealth and the freedom to write.

Passive income online comes from the sale of products or royalties from something you produce. You need to spend time and effort to create something, and revenue may not come in right away. Intuitively, we all know that a new artist with a hit song has probably toiled for years before earning royalties from their music. It is true of any online business model, for example, blogging where one article might take six months before it appears on the first page of Google search results, if at all.

This is the part so many people get wrong in the beginning. They try something and get disappointed when money doesn't come in quickly. And because they need to cover their costs, they quit, often returning to their day job. Freelancing my passion gave me a long runway. I was improving my writing skills and already counting the hours to 10,000. I wasn't earning as much as I had from my previous jobs, but I was covering my costs. That relieved a lot of financial pressure and gave me space to work on long-term income streams. Within a few months, I was ready to take the next step.

Step Three: Choose Your Enterprise

At this stage, you need to choose where you will focus your time and energy to generate passive income. The terminology around business online can be pretty confusing, so I like to split it into three areas:

- A *platform* is a virtual channel on the web, where users go for a particular purpose. Examples are:
    - Amazon e-commerce platform
    - YouTube video-sharing platform
    - Shutterstock stock footage platform
    - Social Media platforms, like Instagram and Pinterest
- *Revenue streams* are types of passive income. Examples are:
    - Affiliate revenue
    - Sponsorships
    - Membership or subscription fees
    - Revenue from the sale of products
- An *enterprise* is an activity that generates passive income. Examples are:
    - Podcasting
    - Blogging
    - Online course
    - E-commerce

It's vital to think about the *enterprise* you choose as a significant project that will take time and money to grow into a real business. Online businesses often look simple, but that is an illusion. Just because you can set up a website or e-commerce store relatively easily does not mean you will make money from doing it quickly. So many people start a project like a social media channel or a podcast believing that in days or weeks, they will have earned income. People would never have the same expectation for an offline business.

The reality is that the enterprise you choose will take time: to set up, to master, and to build a profitable audience. It is best not to try to do more than one at a time, at least not at the start. In the offline world, you would never decide to open a video production company and a t-shirt printing business at the same time. Yet people try to do precisely that kind of thing online all the time. It's critical to focus all of your time and resources on one enterprise to be successful.

You can use more than one platform at a time. For example, you can sell products in a marketplace like Amazon, and also within an Instagram feed. A word of caution, though: it also takes time to learn how one platform can generate significant income. The tactics and techniques required to grow an audience are different for each platform, which is why it is best to start with one first.

There are many platforms and many enterprises from which to choose. The ones listed below lend themselves to the "Profitable Topics" discussed in Step One and are ideal vehicles for many people's passions like writing is for me.

Blogging

In its simplest form, blogging means posting written articles to the web. There are more than a billion blogs and many different platforms for blogging. The most common type of blogging that people think of is a website created with any number of software tools like WordPress, Squarespace, or Wix. There are also platforms for publishing content without a website like Medium.

Many people start a blog as a hobby, and so a common perception is that blogs cannot be profitable, which isn't true. Many bloggers self-report their income to help and inspire other writers. Top bloggers earn more than a million dollars per year[iv]. Nagi Maehashi, mentioned in Chapter Two, is an example of someone who does this. The revenue streams for blogging are typically affiliate revenue, sponsorship revenue, and memberships. It takes time to grow a profitable audience, but there are many examples of success to follow.

Medium.com is one of the new platforms that made me notice the recent evolution of the web. There are close to 100 million readers, many of whom pay a $5 per month subscription. Medium pays royalties to thousands of writers based on the time people spend on their content. Anyone can set up an account for free, and many writers report earning thousands of dollars per month[v].

You might choose to blog if you have a passion that you want to share with people through writing and images. You need to make sure that your topic has a broad audience and that other bloggers are already successfully making money. The easiest way to do that is to search for other blogs and analyze the revenue streams you can see. There are tools like Buzz Sumo, which show popular blogging topics, and Moz, which shows topics consumers are searching for.

I chose to do self-publishing, but my blog www.theindependentyou.com gives me a place to promote my books and other articles. To find out more about blogging, I highly recommend the course that I took, Smartblogger's *Freedom Machine*.

Podcasts

Podcasting is like an audio blog with some advantages over the written form. For many consumers, listening is preferable to reading. And it is easier to collaborate with other people in a podcast and cover one topic from multiple angles. More than half of US consumers over the age of 12 listen to podcasts[vi], so there is huge growth potential.

The primary revenue stream for podcasts is sponsorship revenue. The host of the podcast reads the sponsor's message out, a bit like a radio advertisement. There are networks for podcasts that make it easier to get sponsorship revenue. Like blogging, people often underestimate the revenue potential in podcasting. Many podcasts generate millions of dollars a year, and even smaller ones generate significant income. Revenue depends on how many listeners or subscribers your channel has. Realistically, you need more than 1,000 listeners to start generating income. To be eligible for most sponsorship revenue, you would probably need to have a podcast with at least 5,000 downloads.

Podcasting is something else that highlighted for me the recent changes in the web: followers will pay to support their favorite podcasts through tools like Patreon. Sometimes, this is in the form of a donation, but more and more podcasters create premium content, for which loyal followers pay a monthly subscription. Podcasting is suited to so many different topics. It is ideal for experts in business, careers, or even a niche like home renovation. You need to conduct the same research as for blogging, making sure that a topic has a broad audience that is profitable.

Courses on how to start will help you to choose a topic and find an audience. *Podcaster's Paradise* by John Lee Dumas is very good.

Online Courses

Online courses are one of the fastest-growing forms of passive income on the web because they can be so profitable. In essence, you create the material once, and it might continue to generate revenue for many years after. That is why there are so many advertisements online from people trying to sell a course.

The primary revenue for online courses is from course fees, a form of royalty. Pricing can be a one-time payment, monthly installment, or membership. Some courses earn affiliate income by recommending relevant tools and products.

Like all the models discussed in this book, it takes time and effort to build an audience for a course. Typically course owners invest in advertising to promote their course, most often on social media channels. It makes sense to start with low-cost versions to test and learn first. Try coaching people one on one. There are many platforms on which you can launch a coaching course that reduce some of the marketing challenges because they already have enormous audiences. Udemy.com has more than 50 million students subscribing to more than 150,000 courses, providing an option similar to medium.com for bloggers.

Online courses make sense if you have a desire to teach people. You will be engaging on topics that matter: life problems, hopes, and dreams. Whatever you do, don't go into online courses just because you think the money will be okay.

The best course that I found on "how to build a course" is Ted McGrath's *Message to Millions*. Ted is a skillful storyteller, who even has a Broadway show about his own life story. I found Ted's course very helpful in thinking about my own story.

E-commerce/Print-on-demand

The revenue from selling products is another form of passive income. I talked about my experience with drop-shipping, which involves selling products you probably don't see or touch. Instead, I want to look at an e-commerce enterprise selling products you create yourself.

Making money from creative passions, like arts, crafts, and design, has always been so hard that most people never get the chance to do it. We all know someone who has a creative passion that they have not been able to pursue. But the web today is providing an opportunity for many types of creative people, not only writers.

Etsy, which launched in 2005, is a marketplace specifically for handmade arts, crafts, clothing, and many other products. It has strict rules to ensure you make the products you sell. So, this is a good starting point for your research if your passion is around making and designing things. Etsy is a platform for artists and designers in the same way that Medium.com is for writers. With just a little research, you can find many success stories of artists and designers on Etsy.

Reuben Reuel started a store on Etsy at a time when he had very little money and was desperately unhappy in his job. He said not doing what he wanted to do caused him to cry daily, and that was what prompted him to create his clothing brand Demestik on Etsy[vii]. His designs have become popular, with stars like Beyonce wearing them. And he achieved independent wealth from his e-commerce business.

Starting in a marketplace like this is an excellent way to build and learn. There is a lot to the e-commerce process that you need to master, like pricing, logistics, and legal. Learning without having to invest in a website at the start is a smart way to build an online business. When you are ready to create a custom store, there are many tools and methods to do it. Shopify provides absolutely everything you would need to build a full-fledged professional e-commerce store.

Print-on-demand is a different e-commece starting point for a creative person. Platforms like Etsy, Amazon, and Shopify also make this very accessible. Tools like "Printify" take care of the printing and shipping, which means you can spend more time on design.

Kevin David's YouTube videos and his course *Ecom Agency* are good starting points to find out more about e-commerce as an enterprise.

Digital Publishing

The digital publishing industry has grown in the last 15 years so much that self-published books now make up more than 30% of all e-books. Amazon paid out over 250 million dollars to independent authors in 2019[viii]. In addition to Kindle Direct Publishing, there are other growing platforms like Create Space, iBooks, and Kobo.

Passive income in self-publishing means the royalty income from book sales. E-books are inexpensive to produce, and some authors offer them for free to drive traffic to a site or promote another part of their business. Successful independent authors can grow an audience for revenue streams like speaking, guest-writing, or coaching. The potential is endless.

A great place to start researching is Gundi Gabrielle's course is her book, *Kindle Bestseller Publishing: Write a Bestseller in 30 Days!* and her course, *Dream Clients on Autopilot*. There are also hundreds of websites and blogs dedicated to self-publishing.

Content Creation – Video, Photography

The number of platforms where you can publish visual content and get paid is growing at an extraordinary rate. This enterprise is best explained with examples:

Stock Footage Platforms

Digital transformation is driving the need for more digital content. As entrepreneurs create more and more websites or channels on platforms, the need for realistic, natural footage is growing; in particular 4k video content. If you are an artist, an illustrator, or a photographer, stock footage platforms are a great way to generate passive income. You get paid when customers of the platform license your content, a royalty. Platform companies include Getty, Adobe, Shutterstock, and Pond5.

Jeven Dovey is a poster child for how to start an online business using an approach similar to the blueprint I am sharing with you. He began as a cameraman in the film industry before following his passion for creating documentaries and reality shows. Jeven loved this niche but found it did not pay well. He generated passive income by selling content on stock footage platforms. And then he made a course about how to do precisely that, called: *Creator Film School*

Social Media Platforms

Social media platforms provide another place to make money from the content creation enterprise. There are vast audiences: Facebook has almost three billion users, Instagram over one billion, and Pinterest more than 400 million.

The visual nature of these channels lends itself to photography and video content for lots of different topics. There are many potential passive income types, such as sponsorship income, affiliate links, and selling products. You can also use these platforms to promote assets like courses, coaching, or books.

It takes time to understand and build an audience. Two courses that helped me at the start are:

- Josue Pena's courses on Instagram are excellent. He is a great teacher who has worked with many famous influencers, like Tony Robbins and Gary Vaynerchuk, and improved their social media results. His course is *Online CEOs*.
- *Avalanche of Traffic* to learn how to master Pinterest and make money from it.

Video Content - YouTube

If your passion involves making video content, YouTube is an important channel to explore. It would be an excellent way to test online course ideas or to grow a podcast audience. It is the biggest channel for users to listen to podcasts[ix].

YouTube has over two billion monthly active users. Google's machine learning powers the platform, and at the time of writing, Google is still not filling more than half of its advertising inventory. The potential for growth here is immense!

The primary form of passive income comes from Google's advertising revenue share with channel owners, based on the time that users spend watching content. Other forms of payment are snowballing. For example, fans support channels by making donations, as they do with podcasting. Then there is affiliate revenue, the sale of products using Shopify, and users can now license viral content through companies like Jukin Media.

For a great course and starting point for YouTube, check out *Video Creators* course by Tim Schmoyer

Special Mention: Email Lists

Building an email list is not an enterprise in itself, but is worth mentioning. Email lists create revenue streams, such as affiliate revenue and subscription, but they can be costly and difficult to maintain. Substack is a new email list platform with a built-in subscription model, that makes it easier to build a subscriber base. An email list would provide a complementary revenue stream for any of the enterprises listed above.

Focus, focus, focus!

This list of enterprises is to help you to choose the one best suited to both your passion and your profitable topic. Choose the channel you invest your time and energy into based on what you love to do. If you are comparing one enterprise to another, factors like "degree of difficulty," "level of competition," or "revenue potential" should be secondary to what you most want to do.

Don't try to start more than one enterprise at the same time. You will be competing with people who work hard on their business and are passionate about what they do. There is no way you can match them if you split your energy, attention, and resources across channels. If you master one enterprise and become successful at it, you can take time to develop a second one that is complementary. But first things first.

Back yourself, and beware the internet "armchair experts"

The internet is something everyone thinks they "know a bit about" because we all use it. There are very few real experts, though, and many of them specialize in just one aspect. Self-publishing grew in the last 15 years because of devices like the Kindle and iPhone. Pinterest and Instagram started in the previous ten years. That means we have less than a generation of people to produce experts on all of the information you might need to create an online business.

Beware general wisdom about starting an online business, because it doesn't exist. A lot of the information on the web begins with comparing technology and revenue potential. They mean absolutely nothing if you are not passionate about what you do or don't commit enough time to it. Take your advice from people who are experts in their area and who have credentials that demonstrate that.

It's about the money. Don't start with the money.

People always ask at the start, "how much money can I make?" There are hundreds of thousands of examples of individuals who earn a substantial income online today[x]. How much *you* can earn will depend on your ability and how much you put into it. The extent to which you are genuinely connected with an audience and sharing your message with passion will determine your income more than any technology or platform.

When I chose self-publishing as my enterprise, I believed I could generate significant revenue if I followed the example of successful writers and worked hard. After researching and learning how to start, I could see a clear path to replacing the income I had earned from previous salaries, with revenue streams from self-publishing. So it was actually an easy decision for me to make a tremendous change in my life.

When I was trying to work out how to start an online business, I heard some people say, "follow your passion." I saw other advice to use freelancing to fund the start. And many people showed diverse ways to generate passive income online. The critical element I discovered was to *combine* these elements: Start with your passion, fund your ideas by freelancing that, and choose an enterprise based on what you want to do.

The first three steps in the blueprint will help you work out where to start your independent online business. Steps Four and Five will show you how to grow it.

"What's the Story Morning Glory?"

Once you have chosen your enterprise, the key ingredient you need to make money is your audience. You have to get people to engage with your content or products and incentivize them to come back for more. That may sound daunting for many readers. You may not crave fame and may even be put off by the idea of becoming famous. You might think of famous YouTubers with millions of viewers and think, "I can't do that." That's a good thing! I don't advise you even try to.

There is a category of "internet-famous" people who make money from large audiences that follow them, mainly attracted by the entertainment element. Followers might "scan" or "browse" content, but are not fully engaged. By focusing on an important topic and connecting with people about that, you can build a more involved audience. The type of audience that will allow you to generate passive income, even though it is *much smaller* than those that follow the internet-famous.

The next step in the blueprint is to decide on the message that you will build your enterprise around.

Step Four: Know Your Own Story

Many people who write about starting an online business will tell you to seek gaps in the market. General wisdom for business says that you should do things in this order:

1. Identify an audience

2. Find a pain point; something the audience wants and needs

3. Try to provide a solution or a service for that

I think that's the wrong order. I believe you first need to understand your own story, and then find an audience who will relate to it. To get people to engage, not just follow, and to build a profitable audience, you need to have a message based on your experience and expertise. It has to be real and authentic - the essential you! If you start by looking at what other people need first, you will naturally shape your story to match that. Then it won't be your story.

At the beginning of this process, I didn't believe I had a story that was worth telling, or even enough original ideas to write a book. When I began to build an online course, I planned to share my tech startup experience to help people who wanted to create their startup. I arrived at this scheme by mixing what people were looking for first, with the expertise that might give me credibility. That experience was real, but it was not *essentially* me.

My real story is about how I wanted to be a writer but chose not to do that. As I thought about what I wanted to do with my future, I remembered that decision vividly. I remembered people telling me that writers don't make money. I could picture the 16-year-old me thinking, "when you make enough money, then you can start writing." When I recalled this, many things fell into place. It explained a lot of the frustration I had experienced because I wasn't doing the thing I most wanted to do.

I remembered a marketing conference on the Australian Gold Coast in 2017. I attended as a presenter and talked about machine learning technology. A fashion designer called Leina Broughton came to ask me how she could use the technology in her business. We got to talking, and she said to me, "why are you doing this? It doesn't seem to be your thing." At the time, I wasn't sure what she meant. Later in the conference, I shared that I was trying to do a creative writing course. Leina laughed and said, "That's it; you're creative!" I didn't know what to say. I thought that a well-known designer calling me "creative" was the nicest thing anyone had ever said to me. I couldn't stop smiling for days.

When I sat down to start an online business and remembered that I had wanted to be a writer at 16, everything changed. I realized that this was more important than my experience doing tech startups, which hadn't been my real passion. At that very moment, I literally sat down, began writing, and I haven't stopped since. I wrote thousands of words every day: for this book, for my blog, and on Medium.com. I knew what I wanted to do with my life, and I had a purpose I hadn't had before.

That is my essential story: I am a person who had a passion for writing, but who was waiting to make money before becoming a writer. And now, I want to help other people create an online business to pursue their passion. I want to tell other people they don't have to wait until they have money to do what they love.

I nearly missed this revelation by starting with other people's needs. If I had done that, I would never have started self-publishing or written this book. I think my online business would have struggled, too, which is why I say that Step 4 has to be to understand your own story. If you start looking at audiences and people's needs first, you won't be able to do that. When you think of it like this, a "story" is not quite the right word, because there is no fiction involved. It is authentic because it about your true self.

You might think that you don't have a story, not one that thousands of people want to know, anyway. It's completely normal to think that. But if you have a passion, something you love doing, you will find you have a story worth telling. And when you have that, you can go out and find people who want to hear it. Your story gives you the material you need to build an engaged audience that you will generate income from, even is it is not as large as an internet-famous person's.

Step Five: Find Your Online Tribe

Once you understand your authentic story, you need to find groups of people online who will benefit from it. The term "online tribe" is used a lot today, especially in marketing. A tribe means a group of people online who have a similar or common interest: things they care about, like hobbies, relationships, work, people, or even pets. These interests can be:

- Products and services related to art, design, or other creativity;

- Skills that people want to learn or improve at;

- Hobbies or past-times;

- Problems or significant life changes people want to make.

You can't define an online tribe by demographic information, which is a common misunderstanding when people think about targeting online. Tribes are represented by what they follow. You can think about it as people in a particular state of mind, like wanting to change or improve themselves, or wanting to learn something new.

An online tribe doesn't mean a group of people in one place, either. It doesn't mean the followers of a podcast or a Facebook group, for example. People who are interested in one topic will follow it across social media, e-commerce, and websites. That's important to remember because you need to find them on the platform where you intend to generate passive income.

Sometimes I see people talking about "their" tribe. I think that is confusing. You don't build a tribe yourself; they already exist. You should try to find an existing tribe that numbers in the millions. A tribe that other people are already successfully serving and generating income from doing so. And your goal is to become one of their trusted sources of information or products.

Where do you find your online tribe?

Some entrepreneurs get their business ideas from what is around them or people who are close to them. With an online business, you need to look online to find your tribe. The first and most obvious place is to search the channel you have chosen, like Etsy, YouTube, etc., then other media too. Even if you plan to create a blog, Instagram and Pinterest can give you a lot of information. Make sure to read user comments and reviews. Negative reviews tell you as much as positive ones. Try to understand what makes other online businesses successful.

Question and answer forums like Quora and Reddit are excellent places to research. These platforms highlight topics so you can see which ones have the highest number of participants. There are real questions for which people want answers. Start helping people early on by answering questions where you can; you learn a lot from this process. And as you progress, you can use these channels to help promote yourself and what you are doing.

Summary of the 5 Steps to Start an Online Business

Step One: Choose your passion - don't wait till you have money to do what you love. The internet today presents an opportunity for an individual to create an independent business using your passion.

Step Two: Fund yourself by freelancing using your passion. Practice your craft and improve and give yourself time to build a long-term business. To make money from your passion, you will probably need to spend 10,000 hours to get to a high level.

Step Three: Choose one enterprise on which to focus. If you were to start an offline business, you wouldn't begin multiple companies at the same time. Yet people often do this online. There is so much to learn; each platform comes with its challenges. Choose the enterprise that matches your skillset and what you love doing.

Step Four: Understand your story. Think about what your message will be and what value you will bring through your products or your content. Your story possible starts with why your passion matters to you in the first place.

Step Five: Find an online tribe that is interested in your message. The tribe should already exist and be large in number. Other people should already be running profitable online businesses serving the tribe you choose.

Too good to be true? What could go wrong

If you are still torn and unsure whether now is the right time for you to start an online business, that is understandable. I didn't always do it in my youth, but now I do like to consider what could go wrong. Here is a checklist of issues and scenarios that could occur:

1. The platform(s) you rely on make changes

There are many examples where changes in a platform have negative impacts on businesses that rely on them. Some years back, Facebook made changes, making it harder for companies to connect with followers without paying for more advertising. Many of the affected companies had already invested a lot to build those followers.

We can see recent changes on other platforms too. There is anecdotal evidence that Instagram's algorithms are changing, and some content creators on that platform are complaining that it is getting harder now to grow an audience. Blogging might seem established and even staid in online terms, but the recent news that Wordpress.org—an open-source platform that powers 30% of the world's websites—could be sold to a private company shows how quickly things can change.

I don't think any of this should shape what channel or platform you choose. Change can happen at any time on any platform. They affect everyone, though, not just you. If you are doing the thing you love and getting good at it, if you are connecting with an audience and providing them with products or content that they want, you will be able to react and adjust.

It is worth considering that change and threat of disruption are faced by every industry or business today. If people didn't believe that in 2019, they know it to be true after the events of 2020.

2. **You lose your passion for your passion**

A pretty common fear is that if you turn the thing you love into a job, then you might not love it anymore. It might be a valid concern, and I am not sure that I have an answer. I think you are the only person who can answer that.

I do think it is crucial to aim for growth and to set big goals. I believe that if I am not going forward, I will go backward. I don't think that business allows anyone to stay in a comfort zone for long: there are competitors, trends change with technology. Aiming to grow and develop yourself should be part of your plans. Hopefully, that will continue to stimulate you.

If you change your mind, hopefully, the process will help you to realize what you want to do. If so, then you will probably be glad you started. You will have learned a lot that will help in whatever you choose to do next.

If you don't like the enterprise you chose, pivot! Repeat the process you did at the start. Freelance your passion to cover your costs and fund your ideas. What if the freelancing is killing your passion? Freelance something else! A three-month course can teach you what you need to start freelancing with a different skill.

Chapter Four: Beyond the Side Hustle

The process of testing out different business models and thinking about what I wanted to do took me six months. Freelancing meant I didn't feel too much financial pressure, and that time was critical in finding the right blueprint.

When I understood my story was about becoming a writer, the enterprises I considered were blogging and self-publishing. I did try both at the same time and quickly got stuck. There was too much information to learn, and I couldn't move forward with either enterprise. I chose self-publishing because what I wanted to do more than anything was to write books, starting with this one. I have a lot more I want to write about online business, and I hope that I can help people who are trying to create one.

I have a blog now to support my self-publishing enterprise, www.theindependentyou.com. The blog is complementary, and it allows me to flesh out ideas in shorter blog posts as I think about new book ideas and build an email list. I also write on Medium and try to gear my writing for that audience.

I enjoy the many positive changes in my life that happened because of this blueprint and starting an online business.

I write every day. I get up early and write for two hours before I bike to school with my children. And I write for another three to four hours before I bike back to meet them after school. My daily minimum is six hours of writing on weekdays and 4 hours a day on the weekend. I keep track of how much I am writing, and I can't wait to celebrate hitting 10,000 hours - a few years from now.

I love the fact that I can work from home and spend time with my kids throughout the day. My relationship with them has changed for the better, and just that in itself has made my decision to start an online business worthwhile. And I get a lot more done than when I worked in an office; I find offices are okay for 40-hour workweeks but not longer ones.

I still help one of my freelancing clients, NotifyMe, who launched a communication app for small businesses in the United States. I help to write their marketing content. I love to work with them because they are great people, and I learn so much from their projects.

More than anything else, I have an enormous sense of relief from being able to say I am a writer. At times I suffered anxiety, which I couldn't explain. Usually, I attributed it to external factors, like work, friends, family, that sort of thing. There were times where I would find myself close to tears without knowing why. It would sometimes happen when I saw a media story about ordinary people doing extraordinary things, for example. Now I don't fret about the future. I feel assured knowing what I want to do with my time.

I am looking forward to the things I will be able to do as I progress, but I am not in a rush. I just need to say to myself, "You did it. You're a writer."

Conclusion: If You Can Imagine It, You Can Do It

Sometimes, I ask myself why I didn't start earlier. It took a series of things to happen before I had the confidence to take the leap and create an online business as a writer.

Perhaps the most important thing was that I could see ordinary people being successful online by following their passion and working hard. I saw that you didn't need to build a tech company or do something extraordinary to make money online.

Freelancing gave me the chance to work on my writing and covered my costs so that I didn't feel too much financial pressure. From there, it was just a matter of time and effort to find the best way to grow my business.

When I clicked as to what my story was, I saw how to meet the challenge of building an audience. Knowing my story helped me choose online publishing as my enterprise, and pointed me to an online tribe of people who have a passion but are waiting until they have money to pursue it; people who want to move beyond the side hustle.

If I had not taken the five steps in that order, I would not have been able to build an online business that turned my passion for writing into passive income and allowed me to build independent wealth. I continue to work on my enterprise, which was always my plan. After all, now I'm doing what I always wanted to do.

I sincerely hope that this story and my blueprint will help you on your journey. And most of all, if there is something you want to do, but haven't yet, I hope you start now! The world wide web has reached the stage today where you don't have to wait until you have money to do it.

References

[i] *The Rime of the Ancient Mariner* by Samuel Taylor Coleridge
[ii] http://www.foodbloggerscentral.com/about-nagi-and-food-bloggers-central/
[iii] *Bounce: The Myth of Talent and the Power of Practice*, Matthew Syed, Fourth Estate (GB) (1 April 2011)
[iv] https://smartblogger.com/million-dollar-bloggers/
[v] https://medium.com/better-marketing/how-i-made-11-000-from-writing-in-30-days/
[vi] www.oberlo.co.nz/blog/podcast
[vii] https://www.huffpost.com/entry/how-to-make-money-etsy-secrets/
[viii] https://selfpublishingadvice.org/facts-and-figures-about-self-publishing-the-impact-and-influence-of-indie-authors/
[ix] https://www.buzzsprout.com/blog/podcasting-on-youtube
[x] https://www.ryrob.com/: Ryan Robinson shares his annual income on the home page of his blog

Please Review on Amazon

Reviews on Amazon are the life-blood of self-publishing authors – they help more than you might imagine. To get to the point of publishing this book required a measure of blood, sweat and some tears. I am humbled that you bought it and read to the end. I would be extremely grateful if you can post a review on the Amazon store where you bought the book. I check all my reviews and feedback and consider this a really important part of being an author. You will have my heartfelt thanks.

About the author

Joe France has been working in online technology for more than two decades. He has been part of more than two dozen startups, raising more than 14 million dollars in venture capital. Many of these businesses were sold successfully, including one for more than 20 million dollars. He spent ten years as director on the boards of his companies, helping other passionate entrepreneurs. Today he writes books, articles and blogs for entrepreneurs, especially on the topics of online business and passive income.

Printed by Amazon Italia Logistica S.r.l.
Torrazza Piemonte (TO), Italy